CHRISTMAS COLORING BOOK FOR ADULTS

SMOKEY SANTA

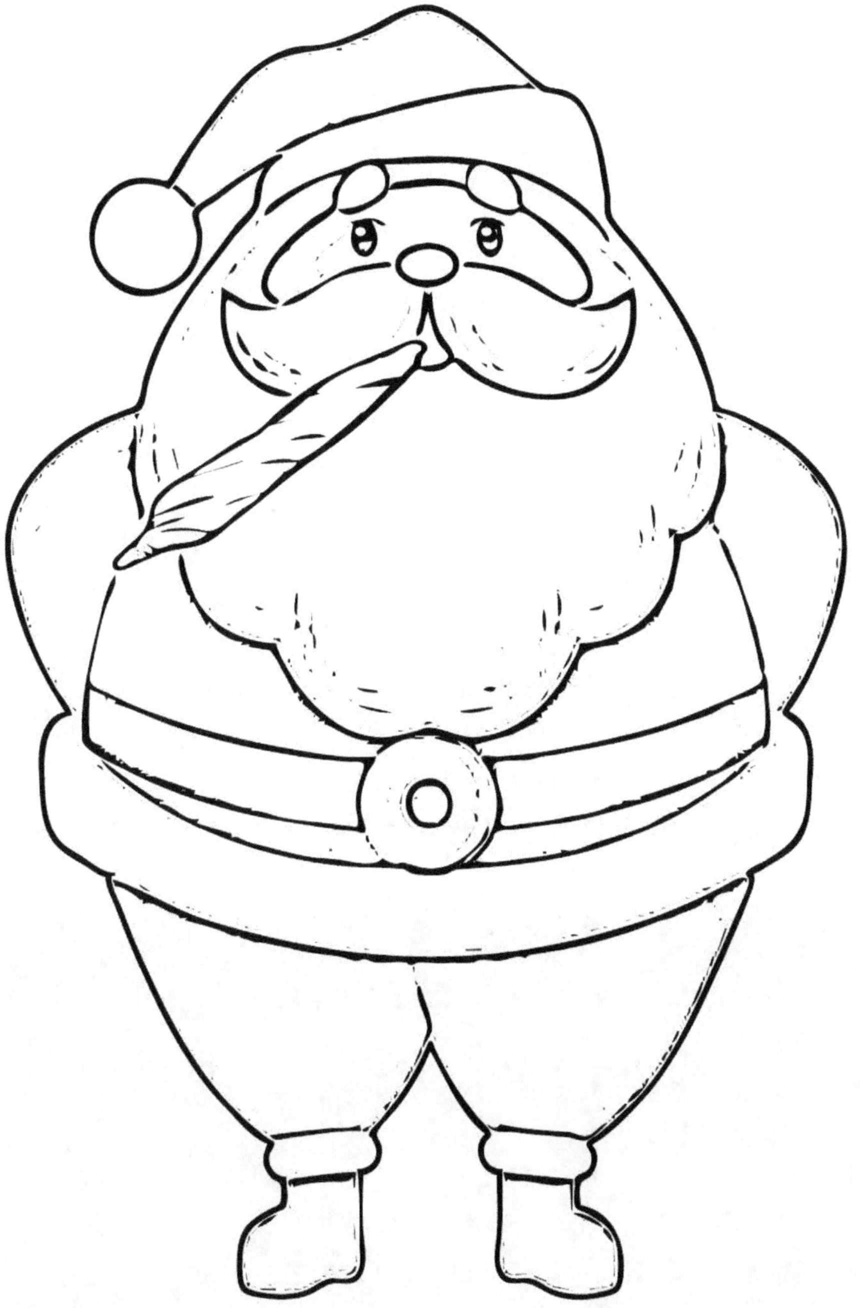

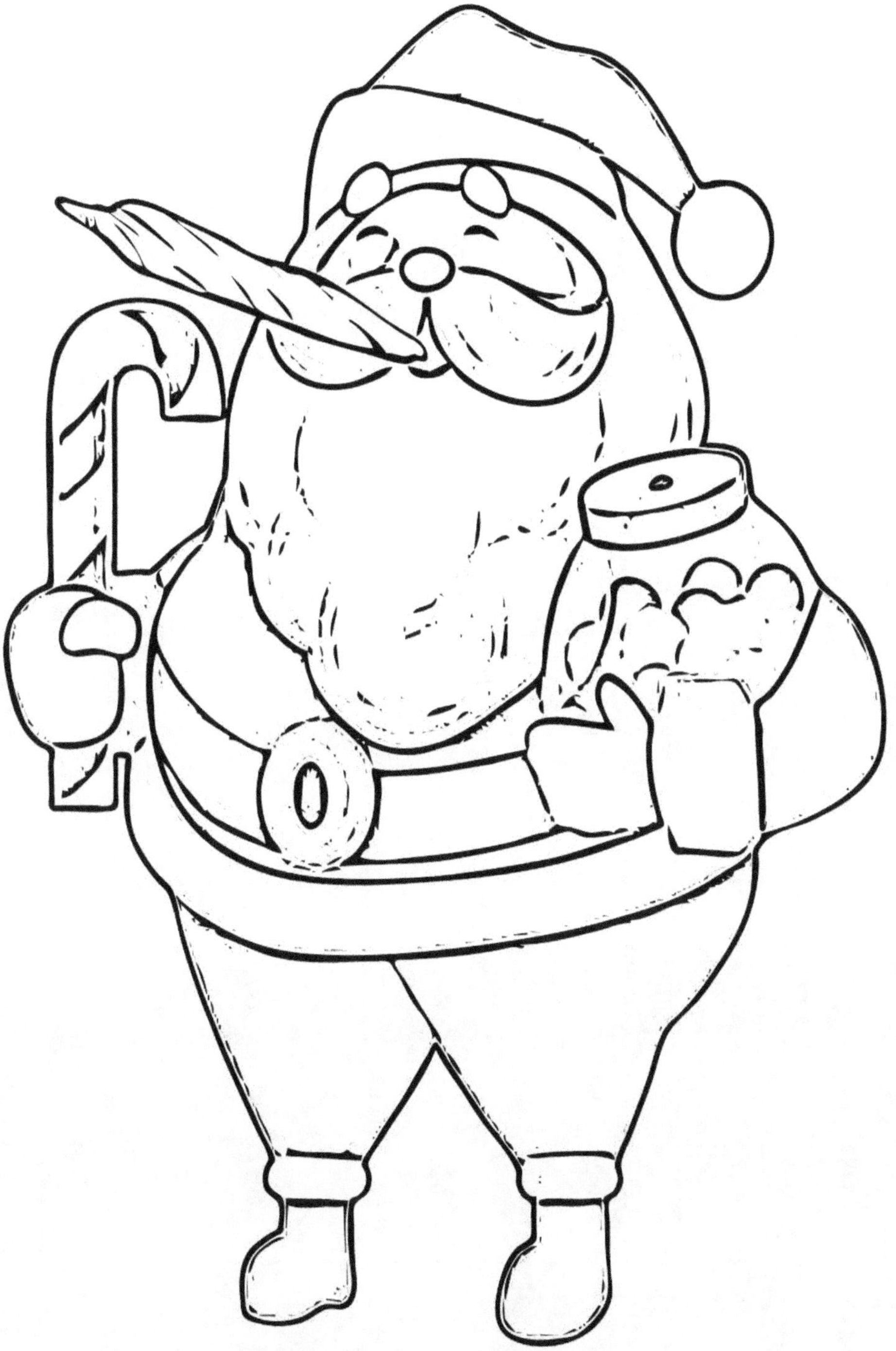

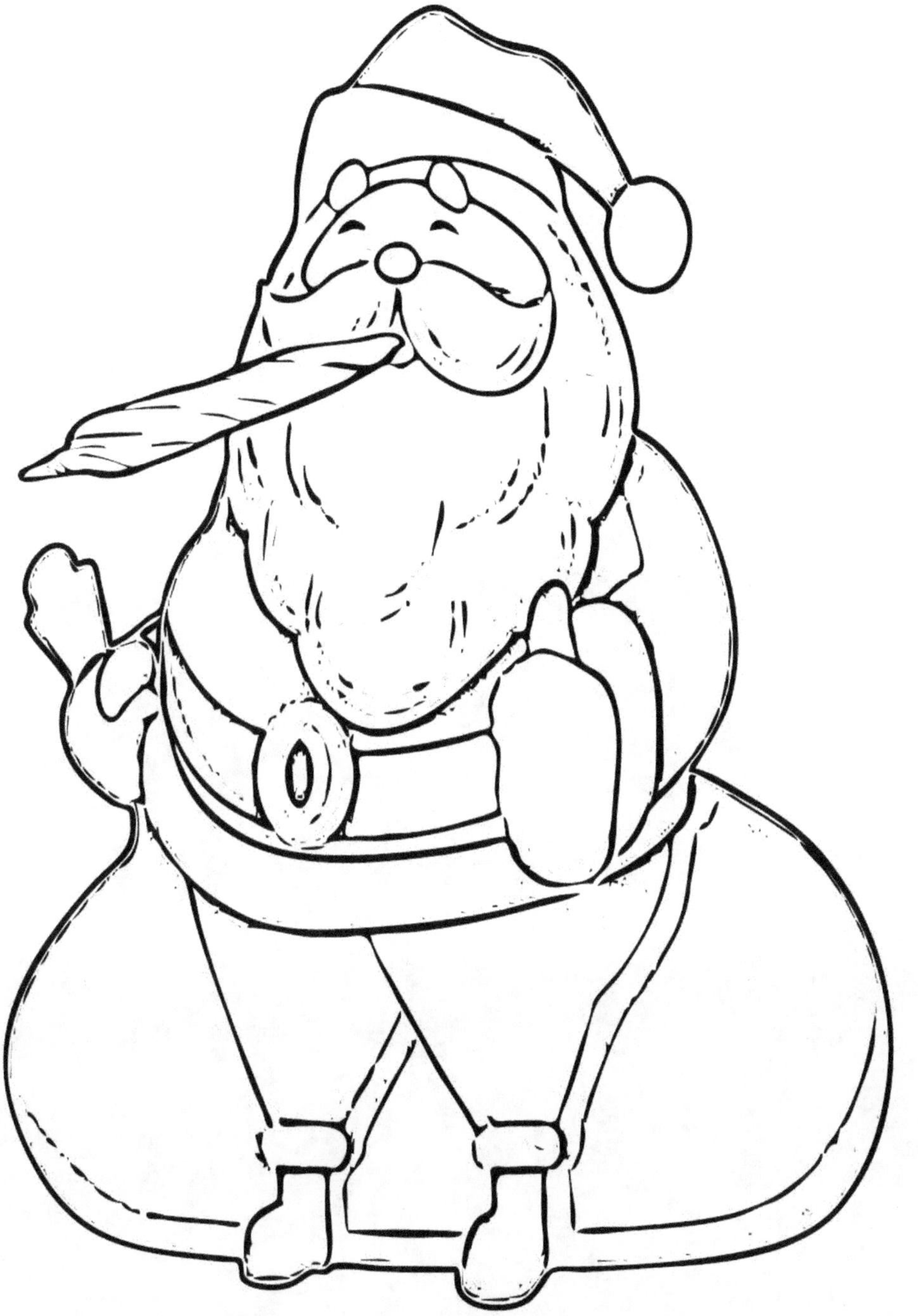

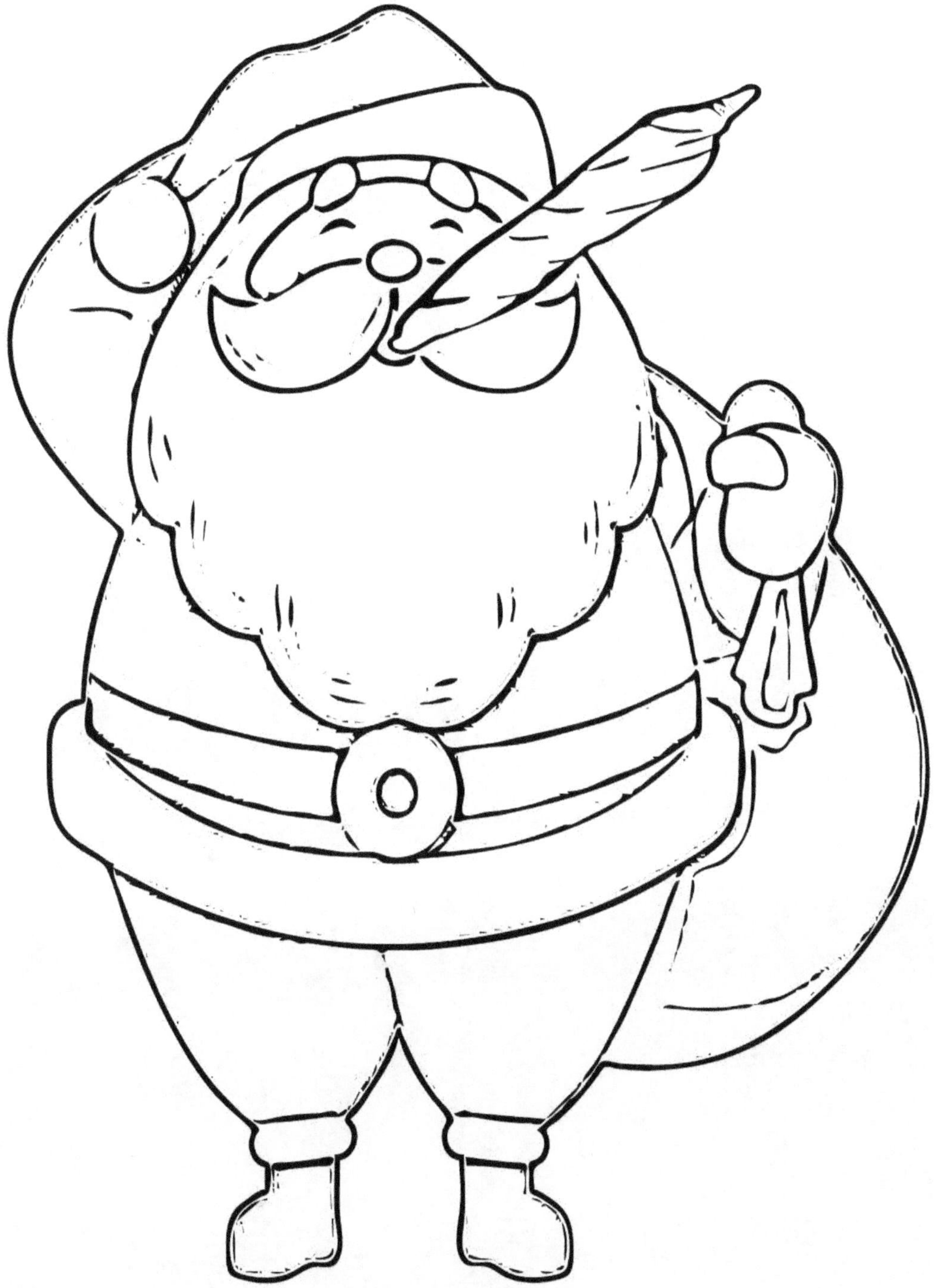

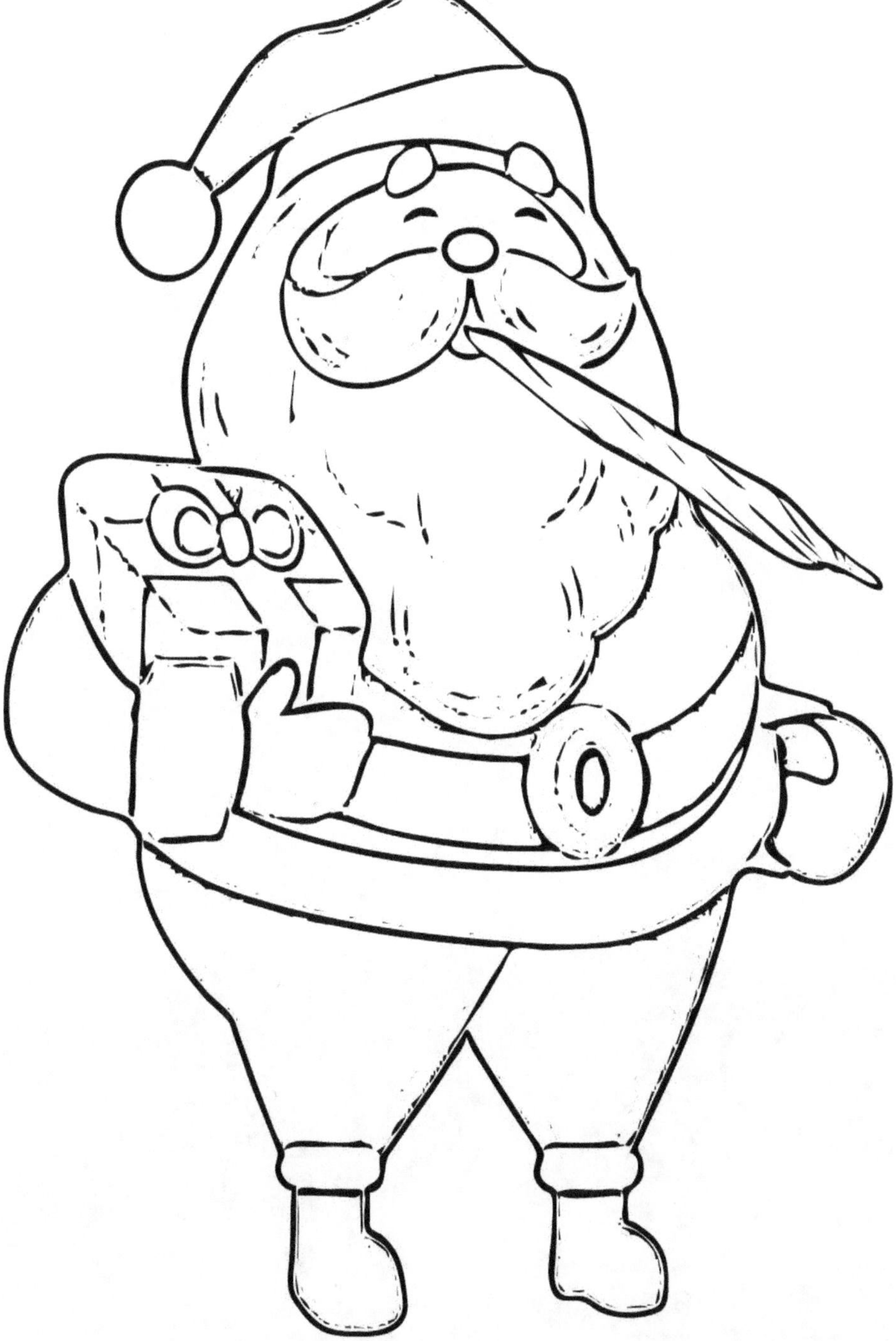

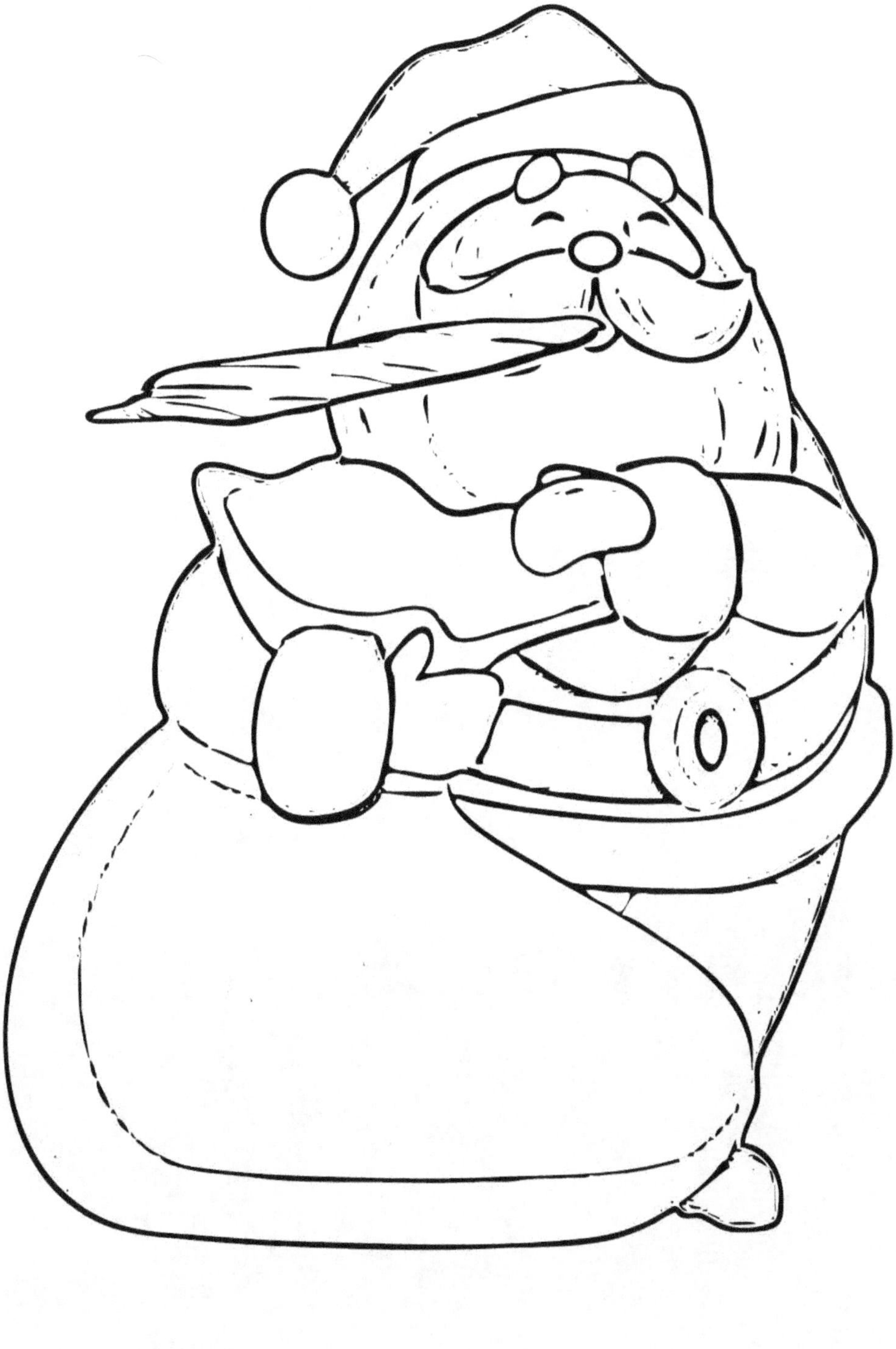

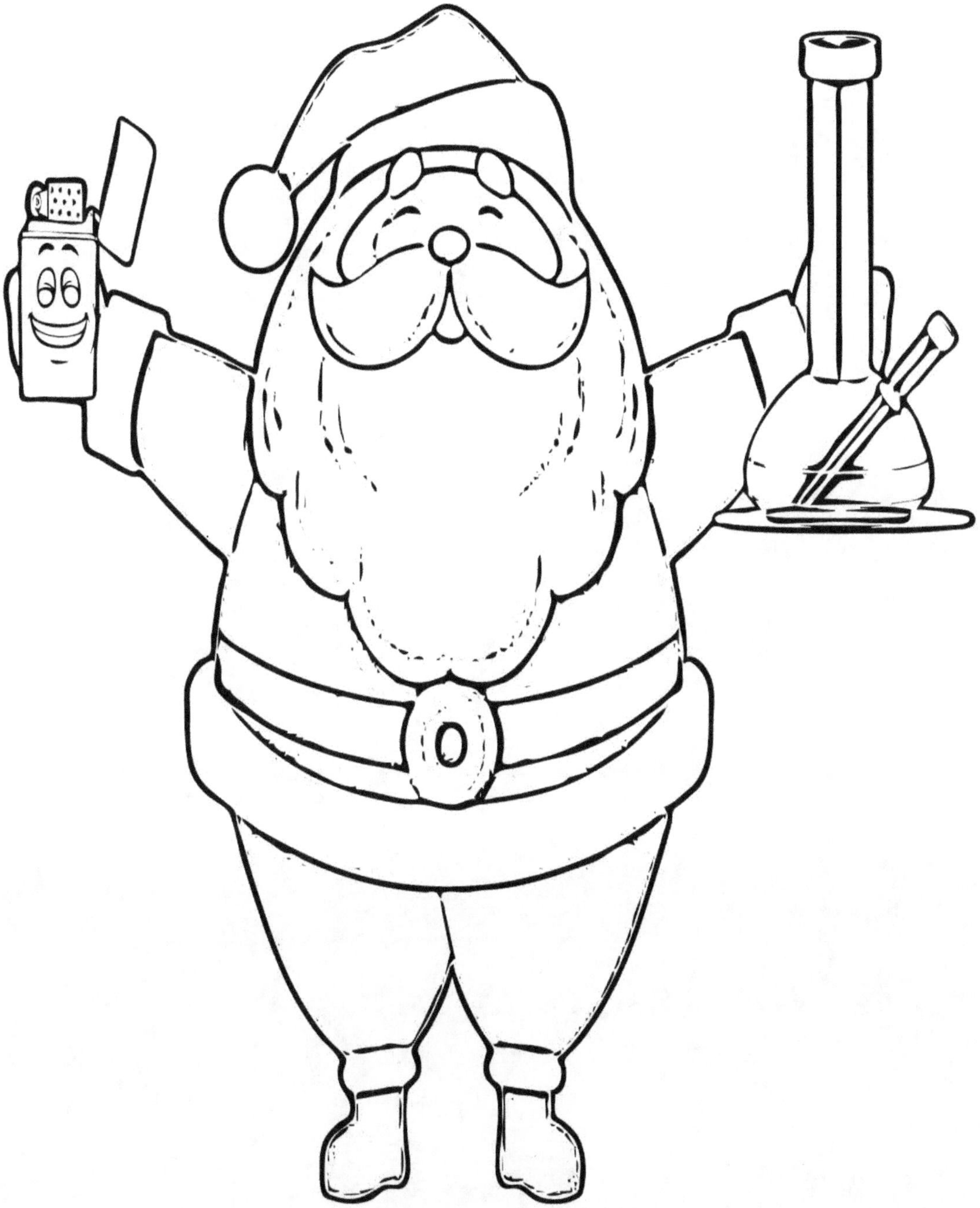

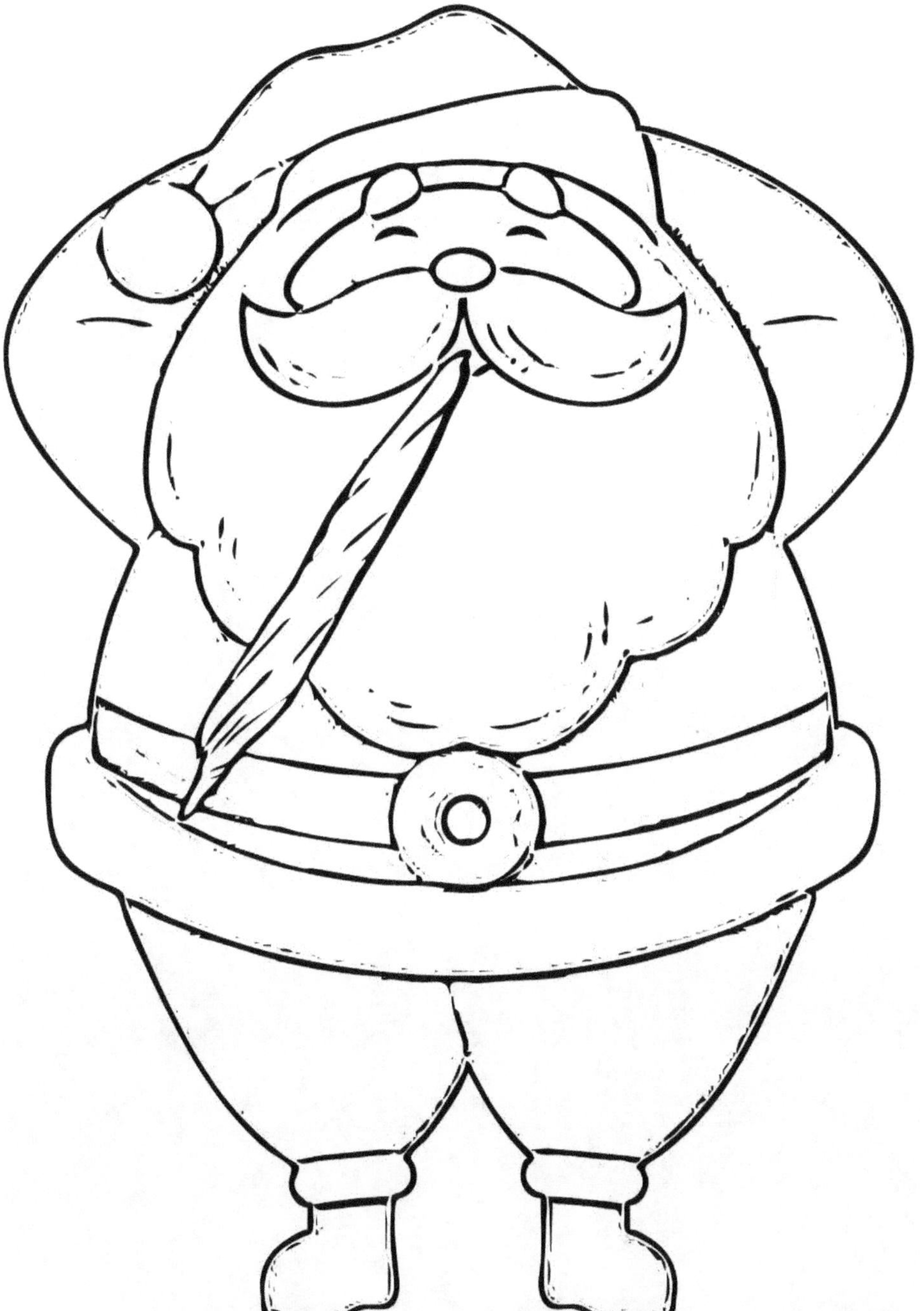

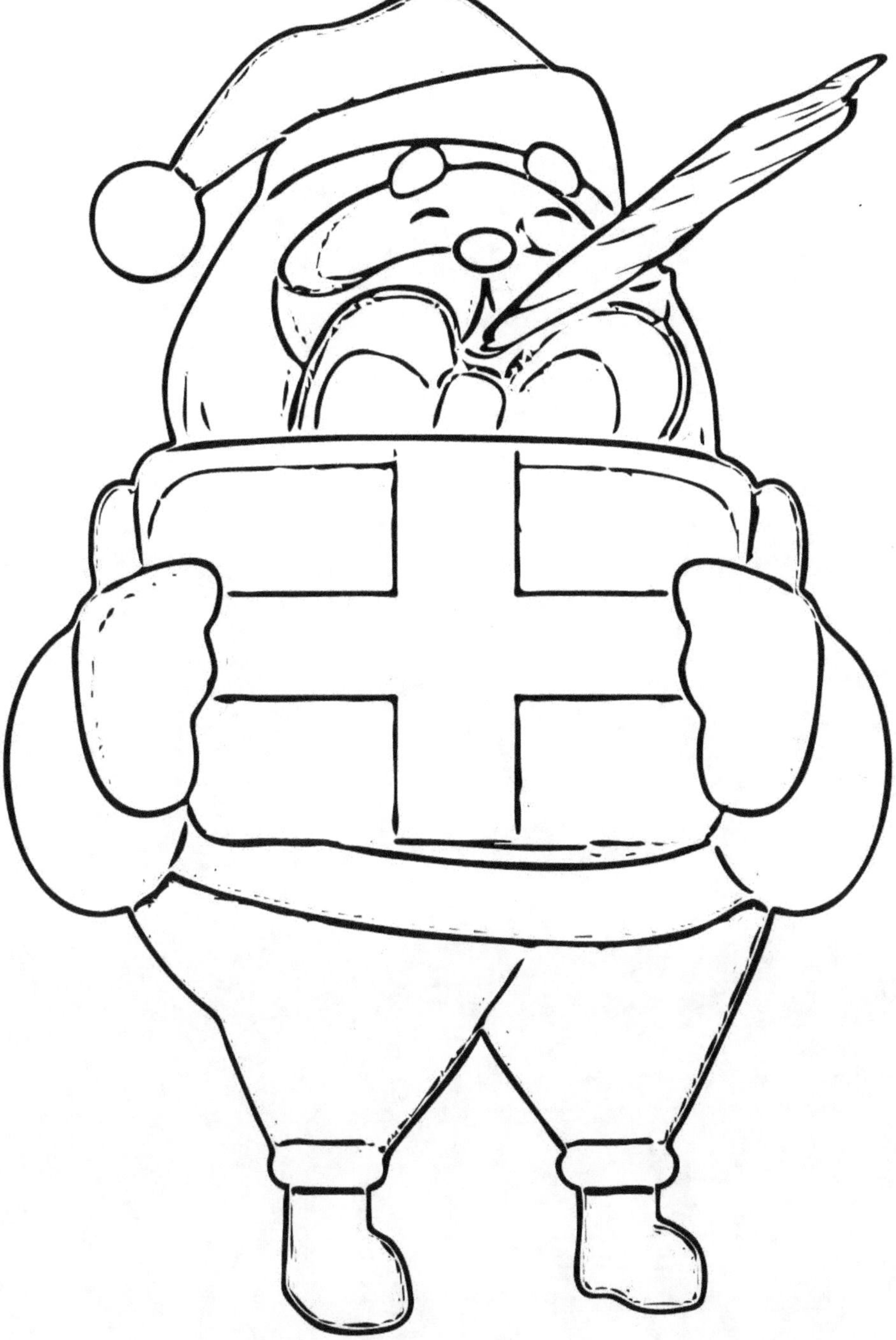

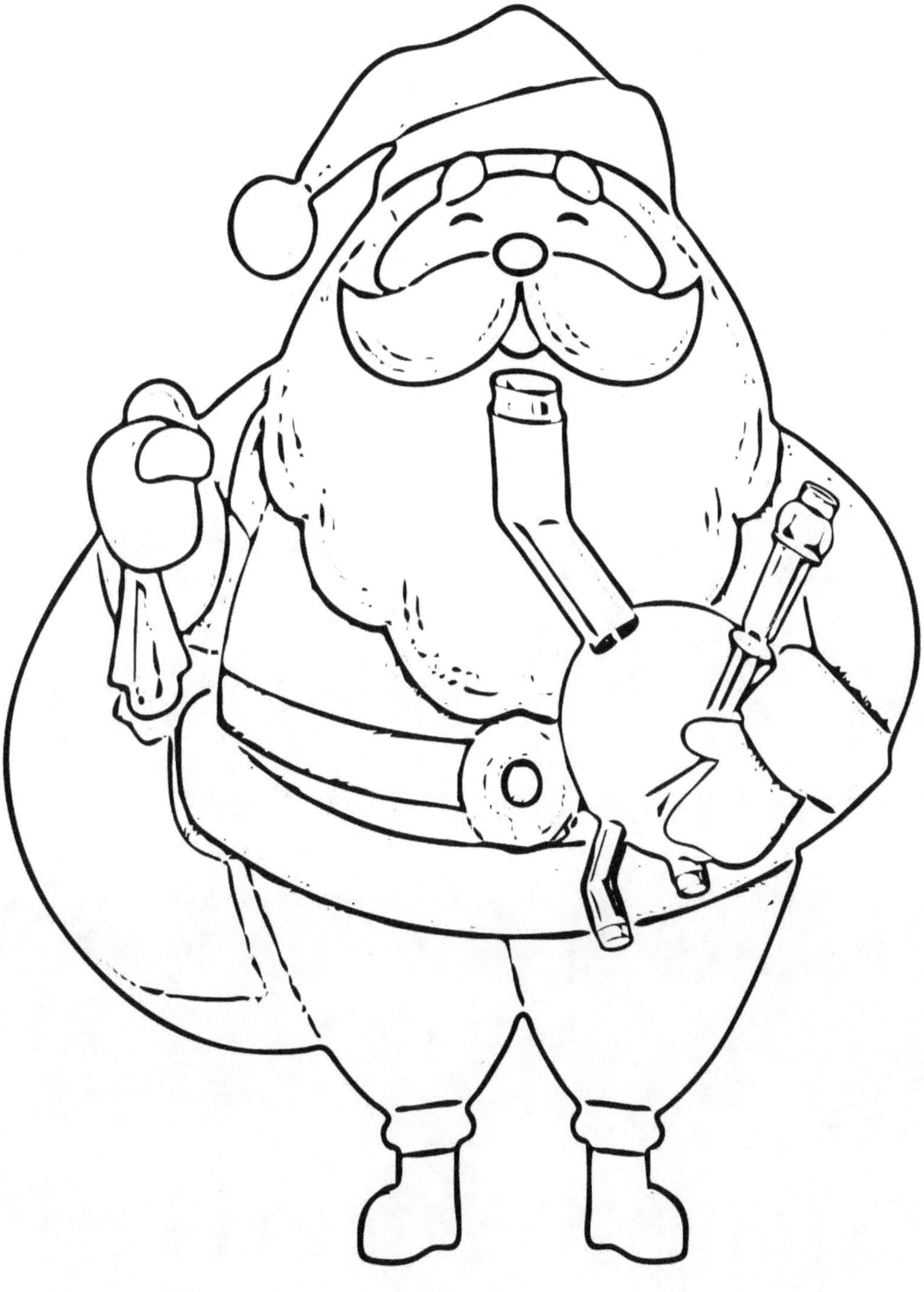

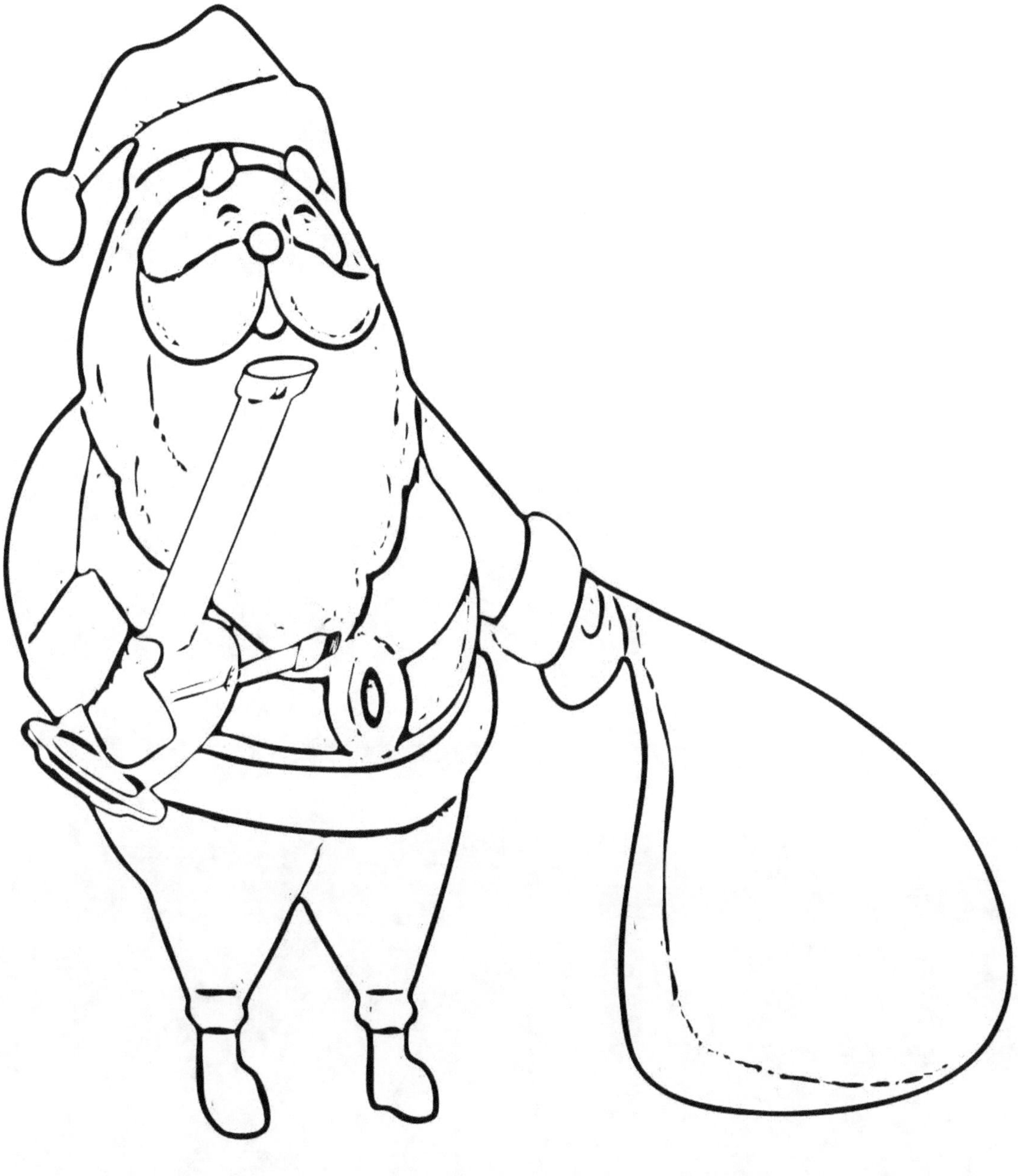

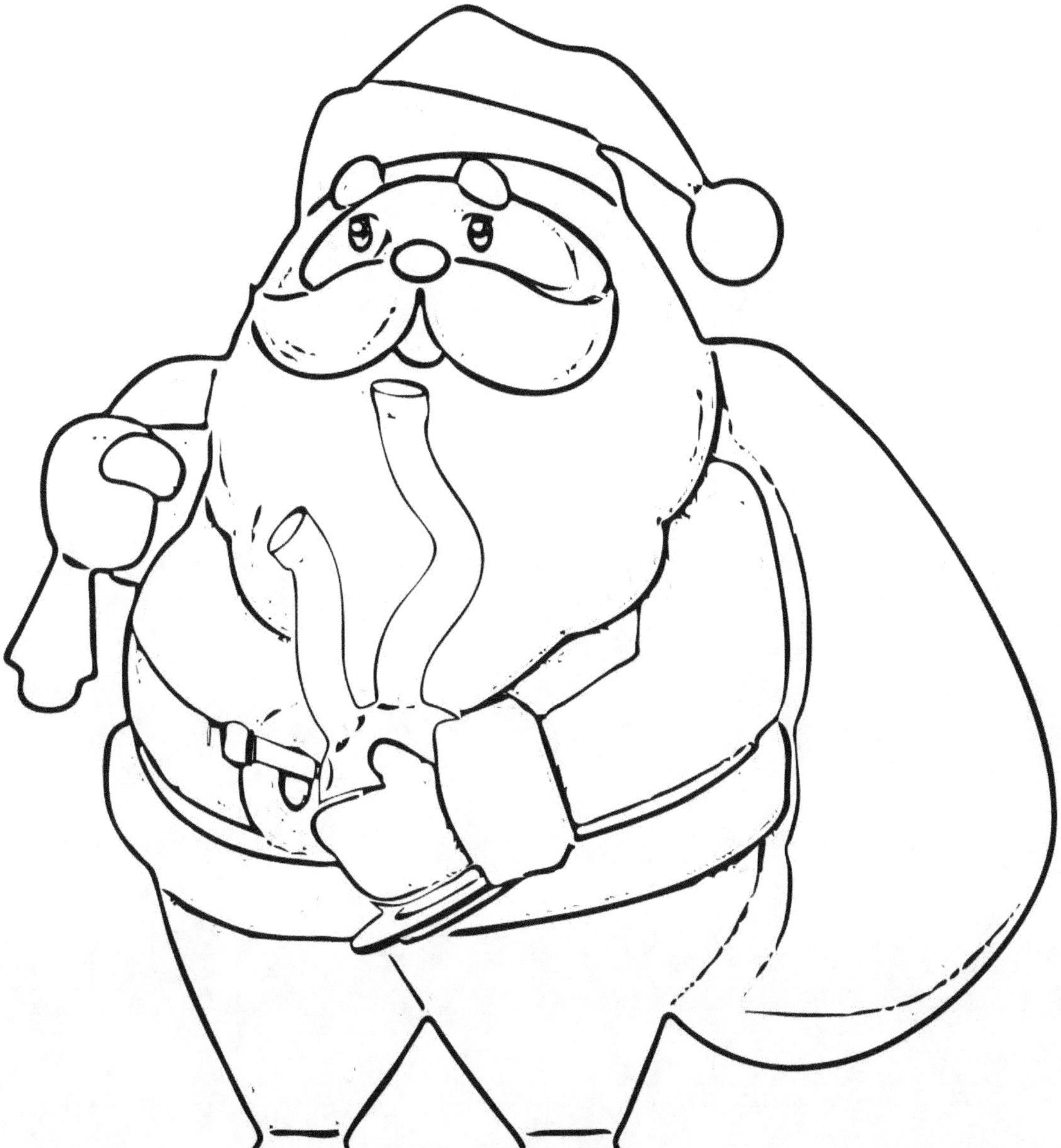

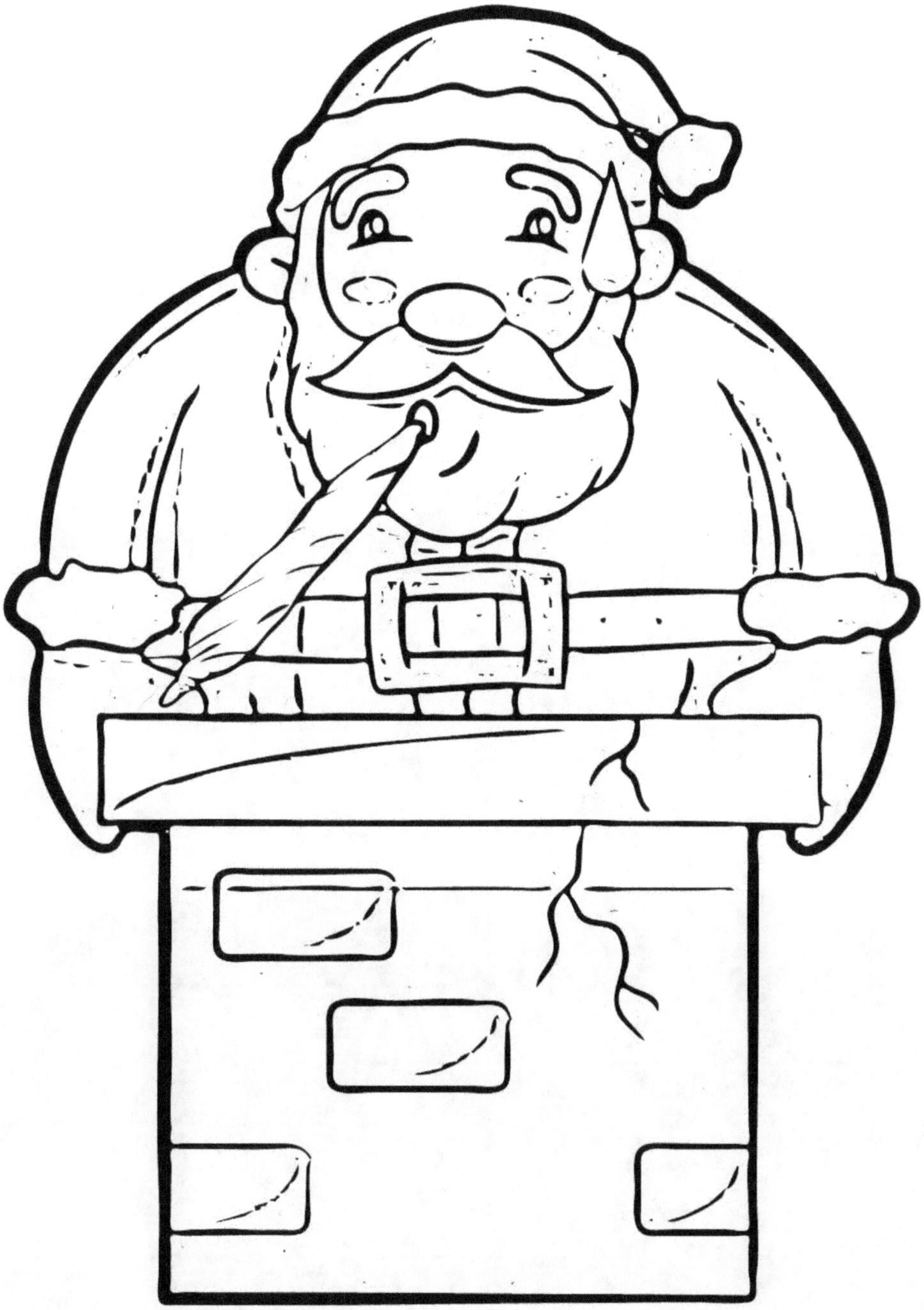

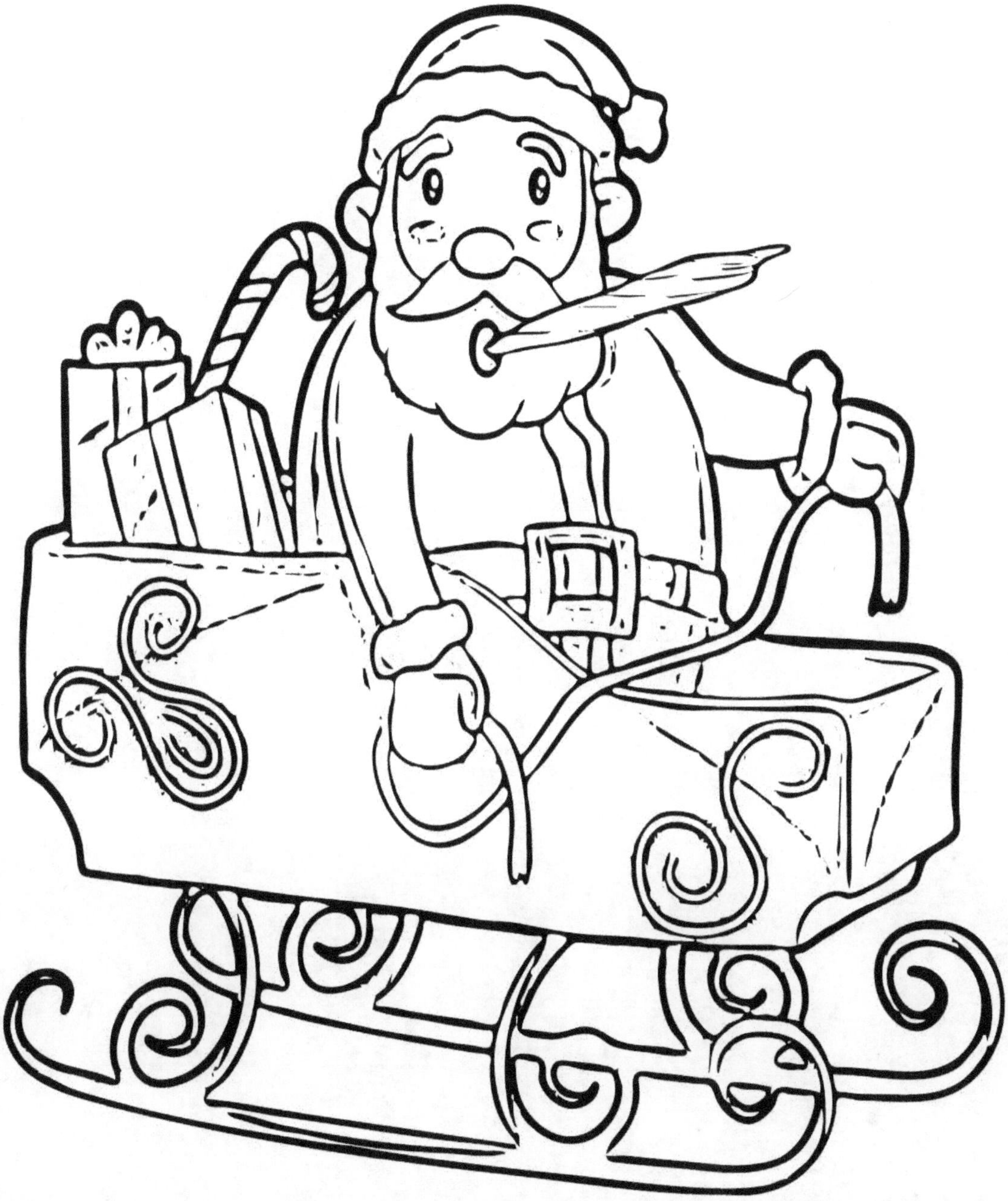

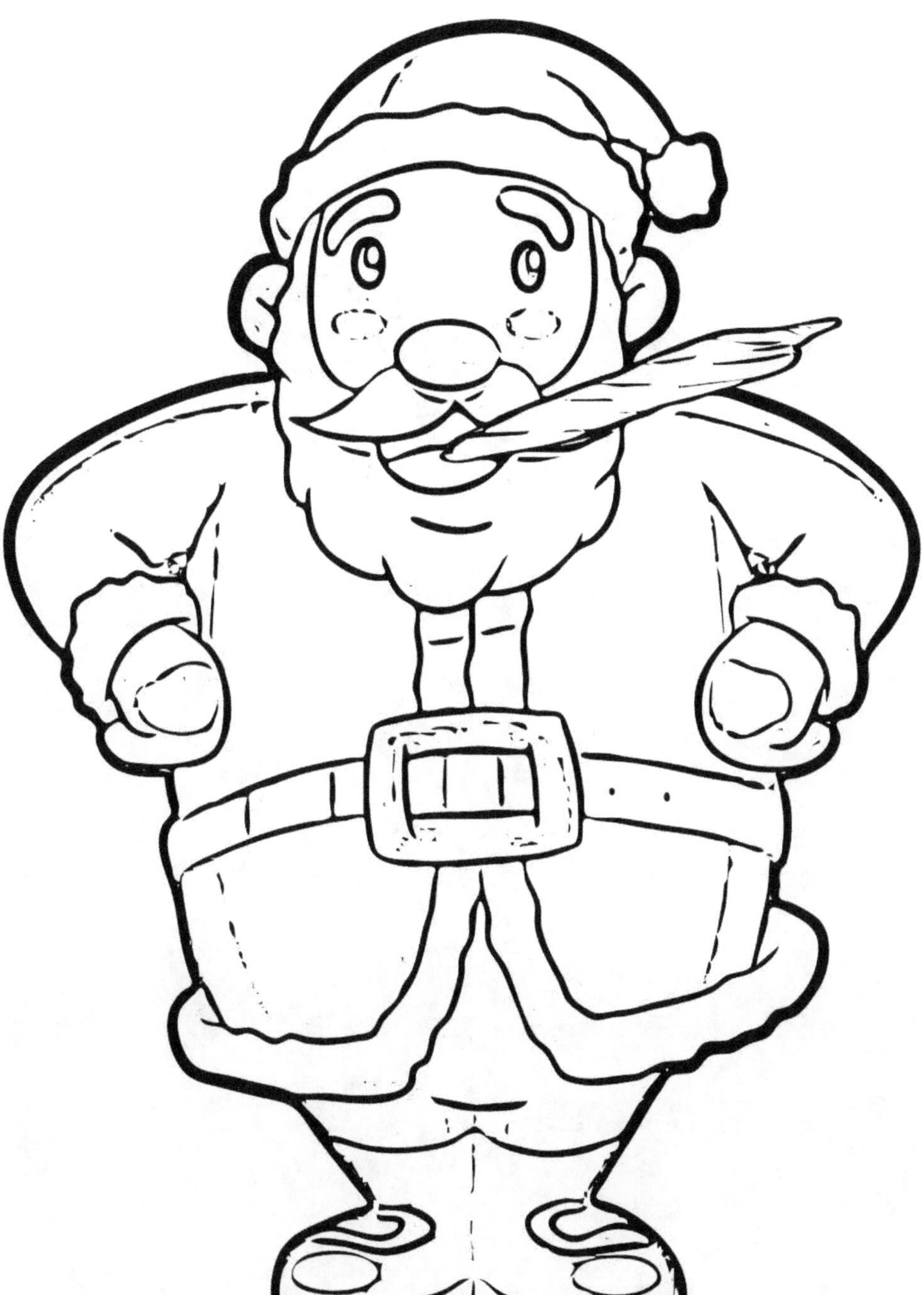

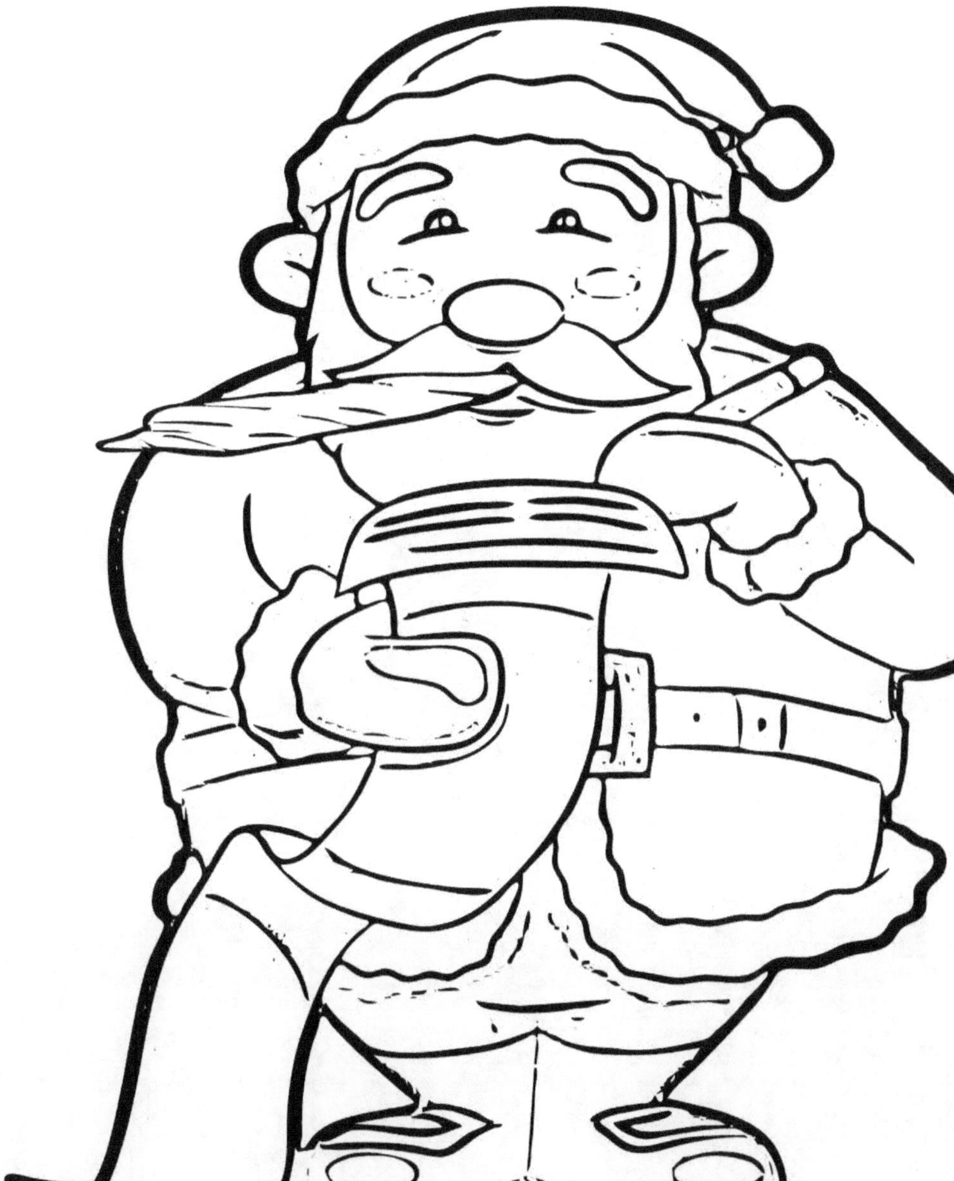

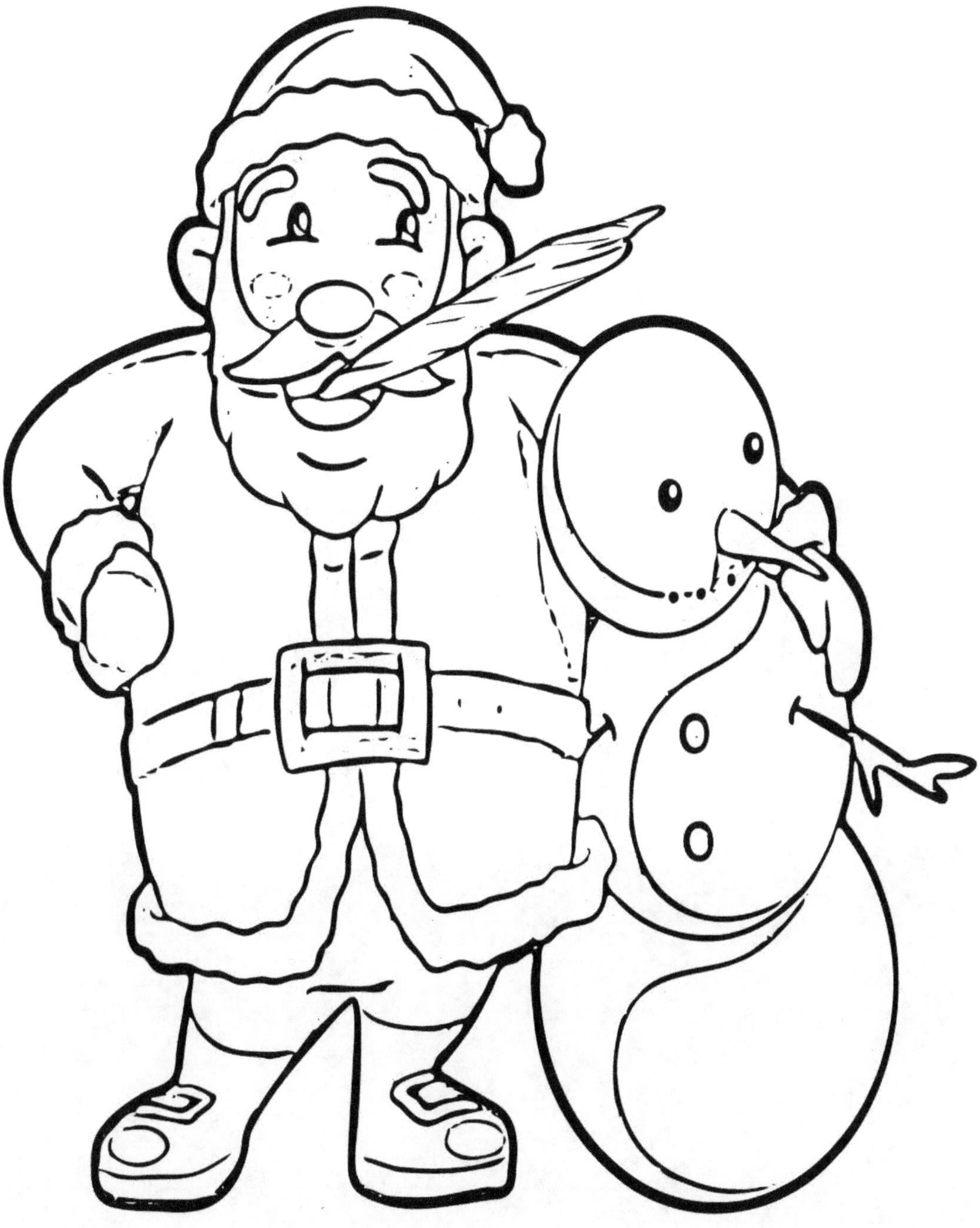

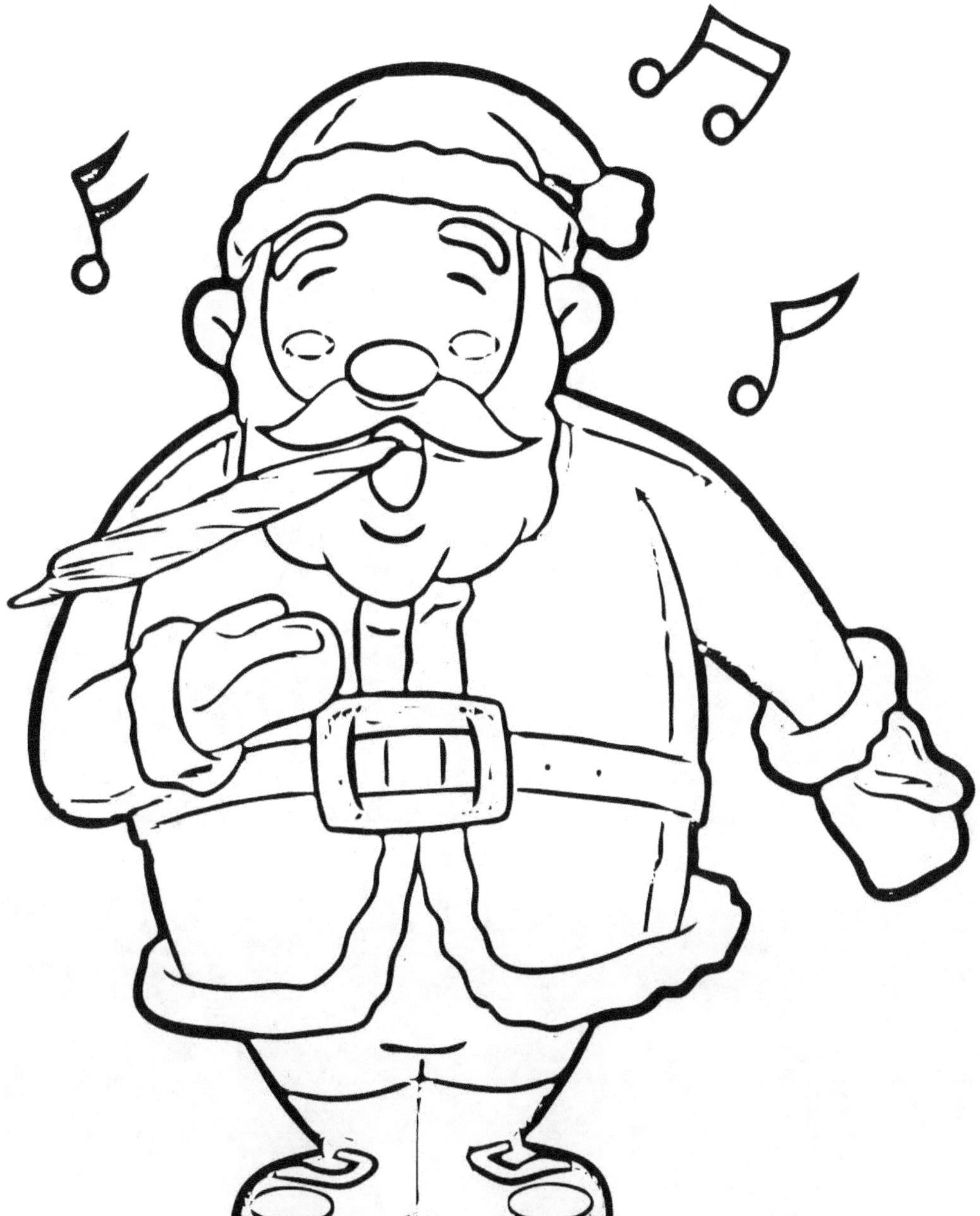

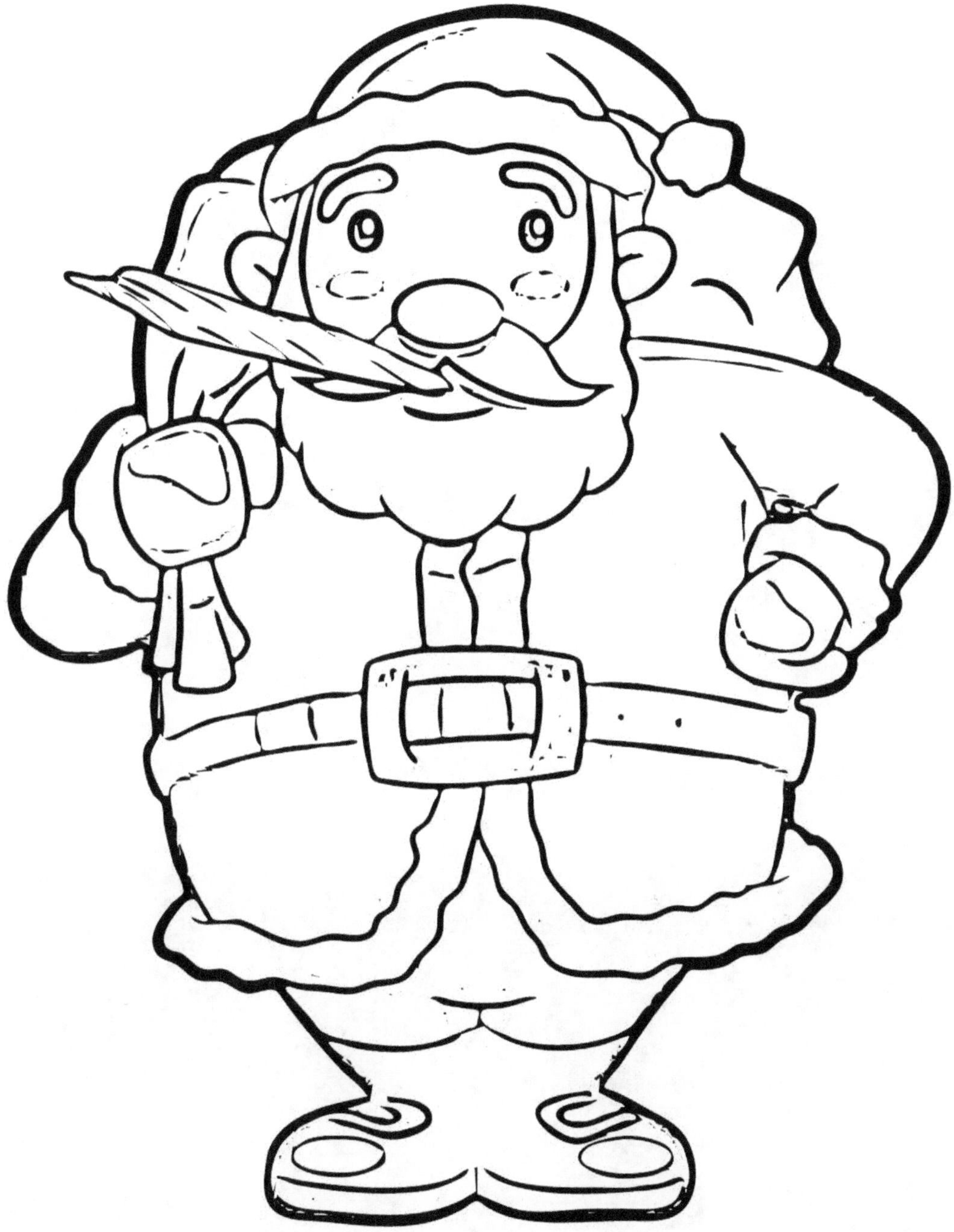

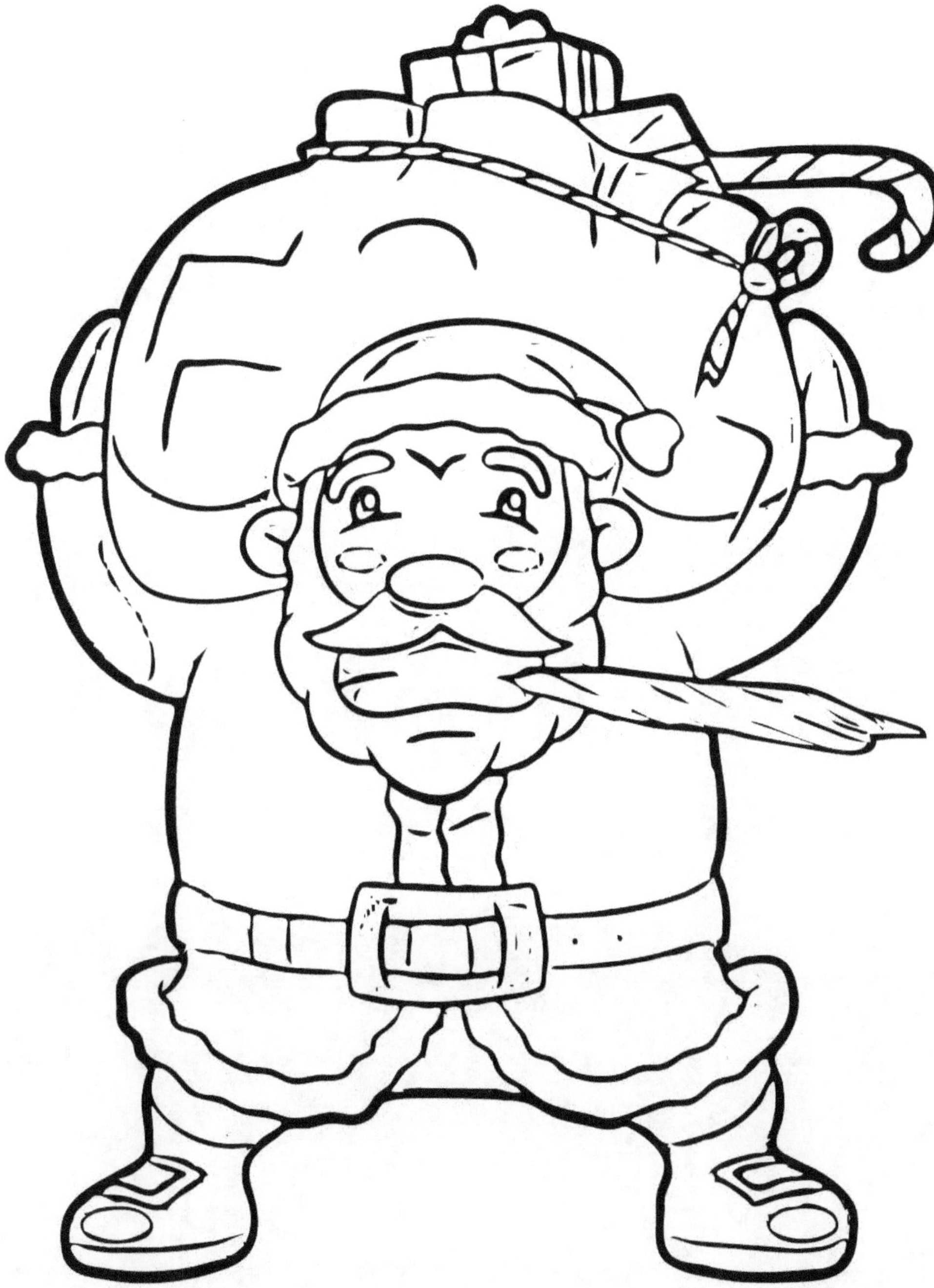

www.ingramcontent.com/pod-product-compliance
Lightning Source LLC
Chambersburg PA
CBHW080617180526
45168CB00007B/2957
9781518774485